The Sun shines in the daytime. At night the Moon glows. Planets twinkle among the stars. Where are the Sun, the Moon and the planets?

3

The Sun, Moon and planets are in the
solar system. The solar system
stretches across space for billions of
kilometres. The Earth is part of the
solar system.

The Sun is at the centre of the solar system. The Sun is a glowing star. It shines hot and bright. It is much bigger than anything else in the solar system.

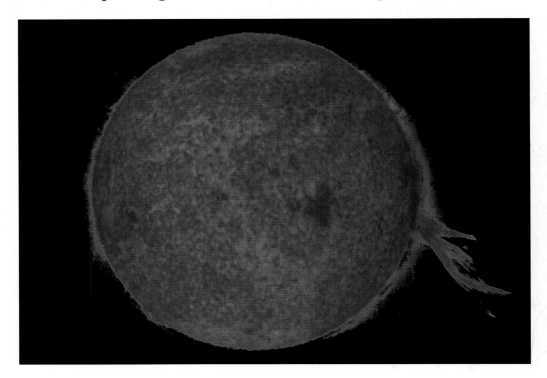

Nine planets travel around the Sun.
Their names are Mercury, Venus, Earth,
Mars, Jupiter, Saturn, Uranus, Neptune
and Pluto.

THE SOLAR SYSTEM

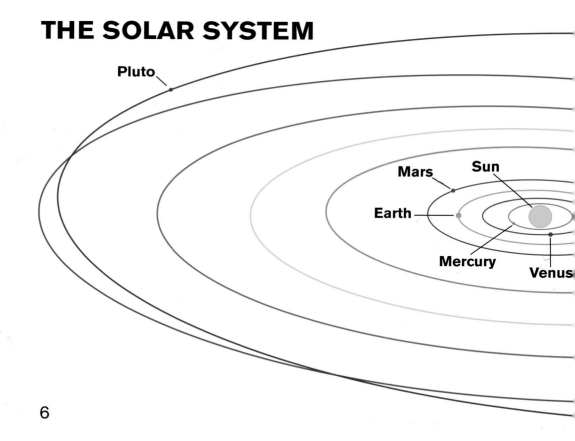

Each planet takes a different path around the Sun. The paths are called **orbits.** Most planets have an oval-shaped orbit.

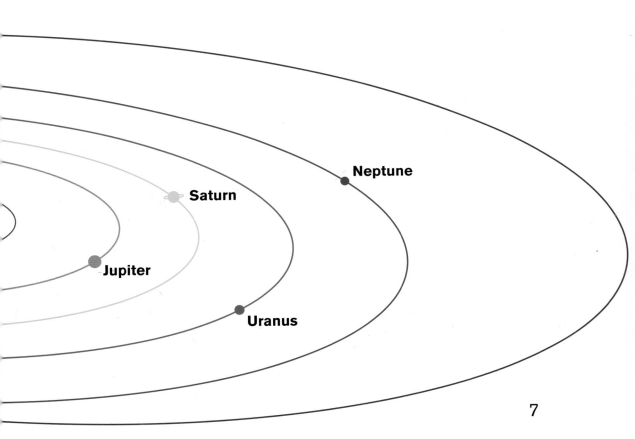

Saturn

Neptune

Jupiter

Uranus

The planets also spin around. This spinning is called **rotating.**

Each planet rotates around an imaginary line called an **axis.** The axis goes through the centre of the planet. Most planets have a tilted axis.

What are the planets made of?

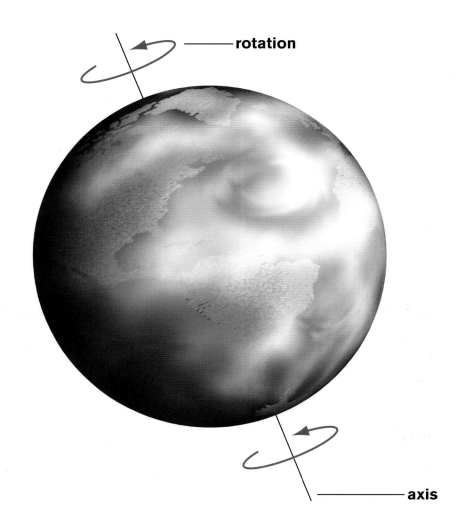

rotation

axis

Some of the planets in the solar system are made of rock and metal. These rocky planets are Mercury, Venus, the Earth, Mars and Pluto. Their ground is solid and hard.

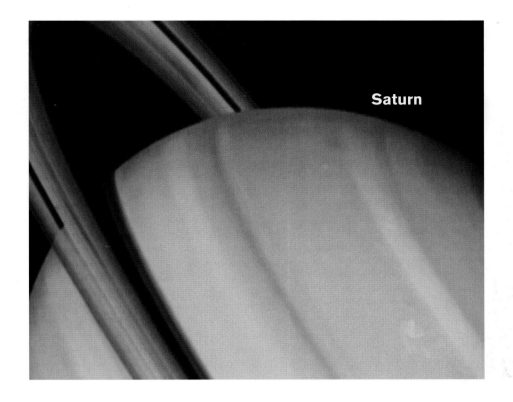

Saturn

Jupiter, Saturn, Uranus and Neptune are made mostly of gases. These planets are much bigger than the others. Each gas planet is circled by rings made of ice, dust and rock.

Mercury is the closest planet to the Sun. It bakes in the Sun's heat during the day. Its ground is covered with wide holes called **craters.** Mercury has no wind, rain or clouds.

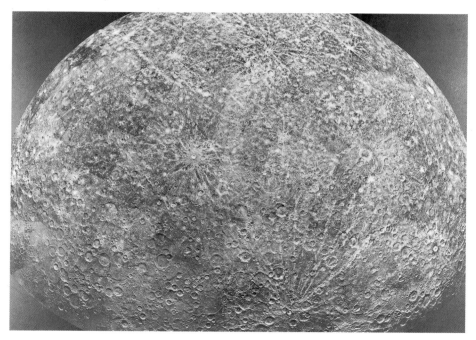

The second planet is Venus. Venus is surrounded by a thick layer of gases. This layer is called an **atmosphere.** Venus's atmosphere traps the Sun's heat, so it is always burning hot.

The third-closest planet is the Earth.
Most of our planet is covered with
water. Plants, animals and people all
live on Earth. It is the only planet in the
solar system to have living things.

A smaller body circles around the Earth.
Do you know what it is? It is the Moon.
Some planets have no moons. Other
planets have many moons.

Mars is the fourth planet from the Sun. It is nicknamed the Red Planet. Red rocks cover the ground on Mars and red dust swirls in the wind. Two moons circle Mars.

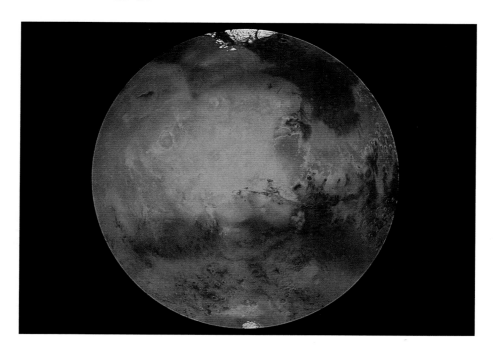

The fifth planet is Jupiter. It is the largest planet by far. Its atmosphere is stormy and windy. The biggest storm is called the Great Red Spot. Jupiter has four rings and at least 39 moons.

Saturn is sixth from the Sun. Wide, flat rings circle this planet. Saturn's rings are the largest and brightest rings in the solar system. Saturn also has at least 30 moons.

The seventh planet is Uranus. It is a pale blue-green planet. Circling Uranus are eleven rings. They are not bright enough to be seen clearly. At least 21 moons also circle Uranus.

Neptune is usually the eighth planet from the Sun. It is a big blue ball of gas. Strong winds and bright clouds whip through Neptune's atmosphere. Neptune has four rings and eight moons.

Pluto is usually the furthest planet from the Sun. It is a cold, icy ball of rock. It is the smallest planet in the solar system. Pluto has one moon called Charon.

Many other objects circle the Sun.
Comets are small bodies made of rock,
ice and dust. They often have long
glowing tails, and they shine brightly
when they come close to the Sun.

Asteroids travel around the Sun, too. They are like tiny, rocky planets, but most of them are not round. Many asteroids travel in the asteroid belt between Mars and Jupiter.

Small chunks of rock and metal also circle the Sun. The chunks are called **meteoroids.** Sometimes meteoroids, comets and asteroids crash into planets or moons and form craters.

People have studied the solar system using telescopes, cameras and other machines. Spacecraft have visited most of the planets. **Astronauts** have visited the Moon.

People have also studied space beyond the solar system. There are billions and billions of stars in outer space. There might be billions of other solar systems out there too.

Imagine taking a tour of the solar system. Which planets and moons would you choose to visit?

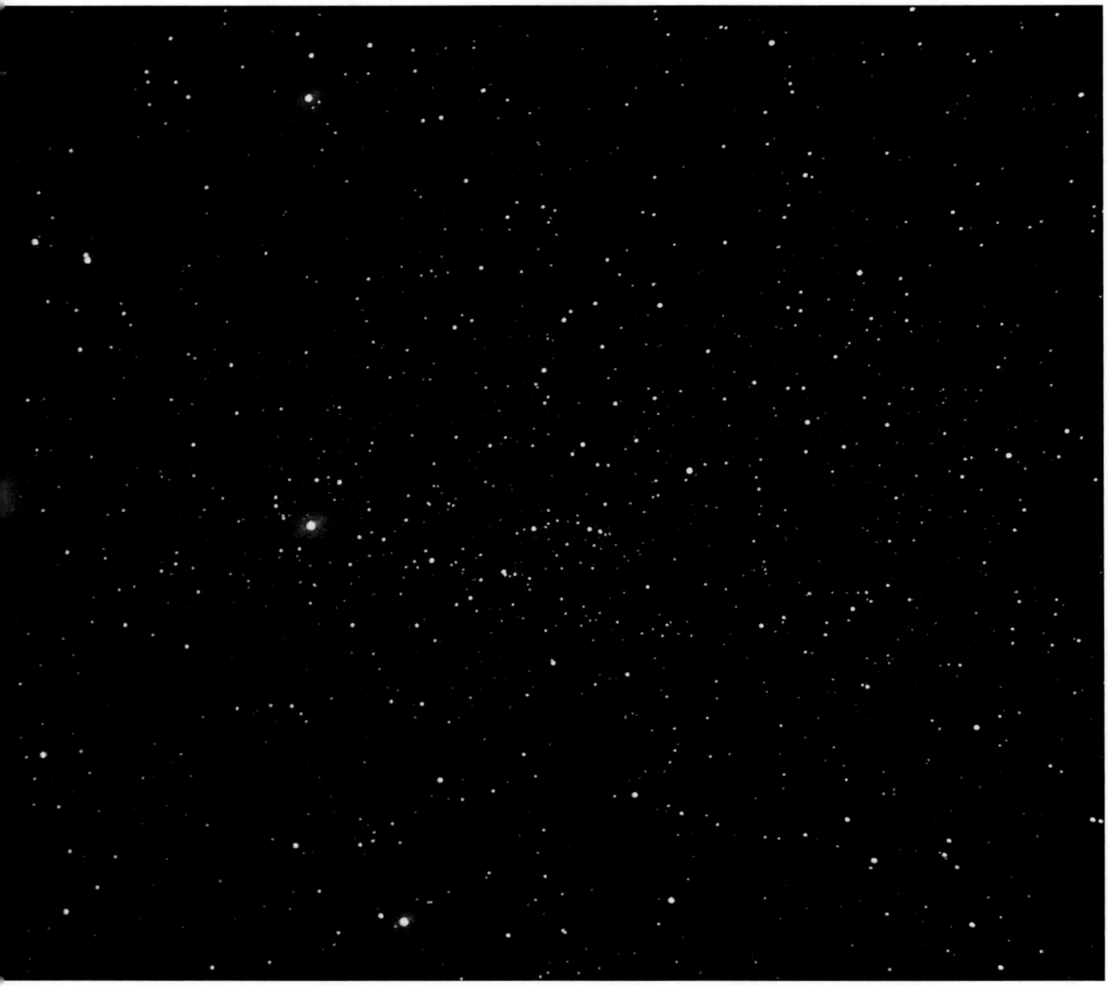

Facts about the Solar System

Planet	Distance from Sun	Diameter (distance across)
Mercury	58,000,000 km (36,000,000 miles)	4,880 km (3,030 miles)
Venus	108,000,000 km (67,200,000 miles)	12,100 km (7,520 miles)
Earth	150,000,000 km (93,000,000 miles)	12,700 km (7,930 miles)
Mars	228,000,000 km (142,000,000 miles)	6,790 km (4,220 miles)
Jupiter	778,000,000 km (484,000,000 miles)	143,000 km (88,7000 miles)
Saturn	1,430,000,000 km (887,000,000 miles)	121,000 km (74,900 miles)
Uranus	2,880,000,000 km (1,790,000,000 miles)	51,100 km (31,800 miles)
Neptune	4,500,000,000 km (2,800,000,000 miles)	49,500 km (30,800 miles)
Pluto	5,900,000,000 km (3,670,000,000 miles)	2,300 km (1,430 miles)

Orbit Period	Rotation Period
88 days	60 days
225 days	243 days
365 days	24 hours
687 days	25 hours
12 years	10 hours
29 years	11 hours
84 years	17 hours
165 years	16 hours
284 years	6 days

Glossary

asteroids: small chunks of rock or metal that circle the Sun

astronaut: a person who travels into space

atmosphere: the layer of gases that surrounds a planet or moon

axis: an imaginary line that goes through the centre of a planet

comets: small bodies made of dust, gas and ice. A comet has a shining tail when it comes close to the Sun.

craters: large dents on a planet or moon

meteoroids: small pieces of rock or metal that circle the Sun

orbit: the path of a small body that travels around a larger body in space

rotating: spinning around in space

Learn More about the Solar System

Books

Furniss, Tim. *The Solar System* (Spinning Through Space) Raintree, 2001.

Oxlade, Chris. *The Solar System* (Science Files) Hodder Wayland, 2005.

Walker, Jane. *The Solar System* (Fascinating Facts About) Franklin Watts Ltd, 2003.

Websites

BBC Science and Nature: Space
http://www.bbc.co.uk/science/space/
This website has loads of information about the solar system.Solar System Exploration

http://solarsystem.nasa.gov/index.cfm
Detailed information from the National Aeronautics and Space Administration (NASA) about all the bodies in the solar system, with good links to other helpful websites.

The Space Place
http://spaceplace.jpl.nasa.gov
An astronomy website for kids developed by NASA's Jet Propulsion Laboratory.

Index

First published in the United States of America in 2003
Text copyright © 2003 by Margaret J Goldstein